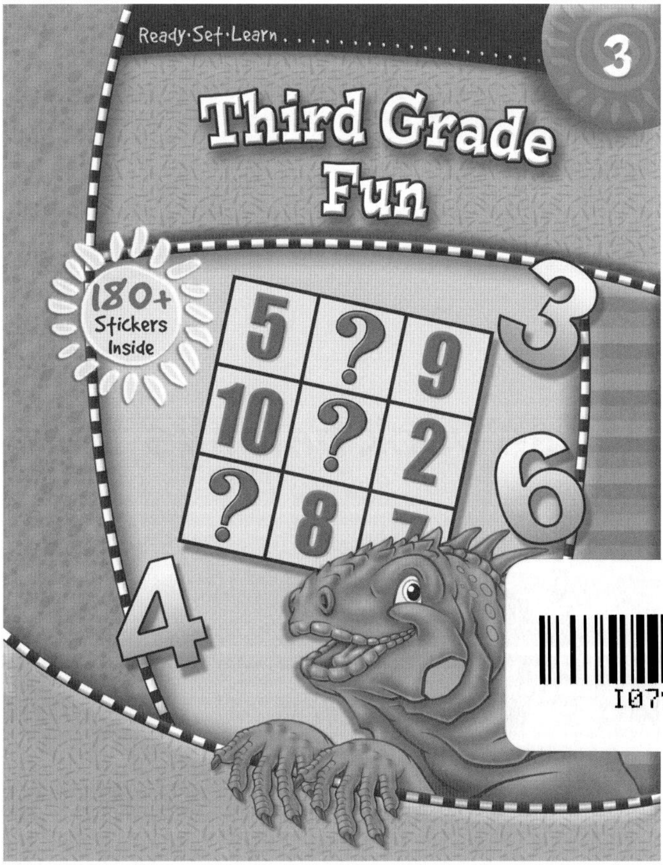

Editor in Chief
Ina Massler Levin, M.A.

Editor
Eric Migliaccio

Contributing Editor
Sarah Smith

Creative Director
Karen J. Goldfluss, M.S. Ed.

Cover Design
Tony Carrillo / Marilyn Goldberg

Teacher Created Resources
12621 Western Avenue
Garden Grove, CA 92841
www.teachercreated.com

ISBN: 978-1-4206-5924-5

Reprinted, 2025 (PO605910)
Made in U.S.A.

This book belongs to

____

Ready·Set·Learn

Get Ready to Learn!

Get ready, get set, and go! Boost your child's learning with this exciting series of books. Geared to help children practice and master many needed skills, the *Ready·Set·Learn* books are bursting with 64 pages of learning fun. Use these books for . . .

- enrichment
- skills reinforcement
- extra practice

With their smaller size, the *Ready·Set·Learn* books fit easily in children's hands, backpacks, and book bags. All your child needs to get started are pencils, crayons, and colored pencils.

A full sheet of colorful stickers is included. Use these stickers for . . .

- decorating pages
- rewarding outstanding effort
- keeping track of completed pages

Celebrate your child's progress by using these stickers on the reward chart located on the inside cover. The blue-ribbon sticker fits perfectly on the certificate on page 64.

With *Ready·Set·Learn* and a little encouragement, your child will be on the fast track to learning fun!

Your Own Information

Directions: Use cursive writing to answer each question with your own important information.

1. What is your full name?

____

2. What is your address?

____

____

____

3. When is your birthday?

____

4. What are your favorite things to do?

____

____

Sports Sorts

Directions: The following words can be sorted into four categories. Each word can be used only one time.

ace	goal posts	shortstop	touchdown
bat	goalie	racquet	Wimbledon
centerfield	helmet	Super Bowl	World Cup
court	mitt	serve	World Series
face mask	penalty kick	shin guards	yellow card

baseball

1. ______________________
2. ______________________
3. ______________________
4. ______________________
5. ______________________

soccer

1. ______________________
2. ______________________
3. ______________________
4. ______________________
5. ______________________

football

1. ______________________
2. ______________________
3. ______________________
4. ______________________
5. ______________________

tennis

1. ______________________
2. ______________________
3. ______________________
4. ______________________
5. ______________________

Ready·Set·Learn

Which Is It?

Directions: Read the number sentences. Add the correct math sign to each problem.

+	–	x	÷
add	**subtract**	**multiply**	**divide**

1. 5 ☐ 7 = 12

2. 24 ☐ 4 = 6

3. 9 ☐ 3 = 12

4. 18 ☐ 6 = 12

5. 4 ☐ 9 = 13

6. 4 ☐ 9 = 36

7. 10 ☐ 8 = 80

8. 15 ☐ 5 = 3

9. 11 ☐ 4 = 7

10. 8 ☐ 16 = 24

11. 2 ☐ 8 = 16

12. 3 ☐ 2 = 5

Magic Squares

Directions: Long ago, people in China came up with a math puzzle called magic squares. Solve each magic square.

1. Using each number once, place numbers in the open boxes to make all rows (across, down, and diagonally) add up to 24.

	8	7
4		
	10	5

2. Using each number once, place three numbers in the open boxes to make all rows (across, down, and diagonally) add up to 18.

5		9
10		2
	8	7

3. Using each number once, place numbers in the open boxes to make all rows (across, down, and diagonally) add up to 15.

6		2
	5	9
	3	

Coloring Synonyms

Directions: Take a look at the flowers below. There are eight pairs of synonyms. Color the flowers with matching synonyms the same color.

Antonym Match-Up

Directions: Draw a line to connect the antonyms.

1.	happy	young
2.	brave	far
3.	right	afraid
4.	fast	weak
5.	big	little
6.	rude	tame
7.	old	sad
8.	strong	answer
9.	crowded	ugly
10.	smile	frown
11.	close	slow
12.	loud	wrong
13.	ask	easy
14.	wild	quiet
15.	beautiful	empty
16.	hard	polite

Word Family Fun

Directions: Complete each sentence with a word in the given word family.

1. The baseball player was up to ________________.
-at

2. Don't go in the ________________ without an umbrella. *-ain*

3. What time did you ________________ up this morning? *-ake*

4. What did you ________________?
-ay

5. I love the smell of the orange ________________.
-eel

6. This toy is yours to ________________.
-eep

7. My little sister learned to count to ________________.
-en

8. Why did you ________________ at me?
-ell

9. I went camping and slept in a ________________.
-ent

10. That's a beautiful gold ________________.
-ing

Compound Gum

Directions: Color the pieces of gum that have compound words written on them.

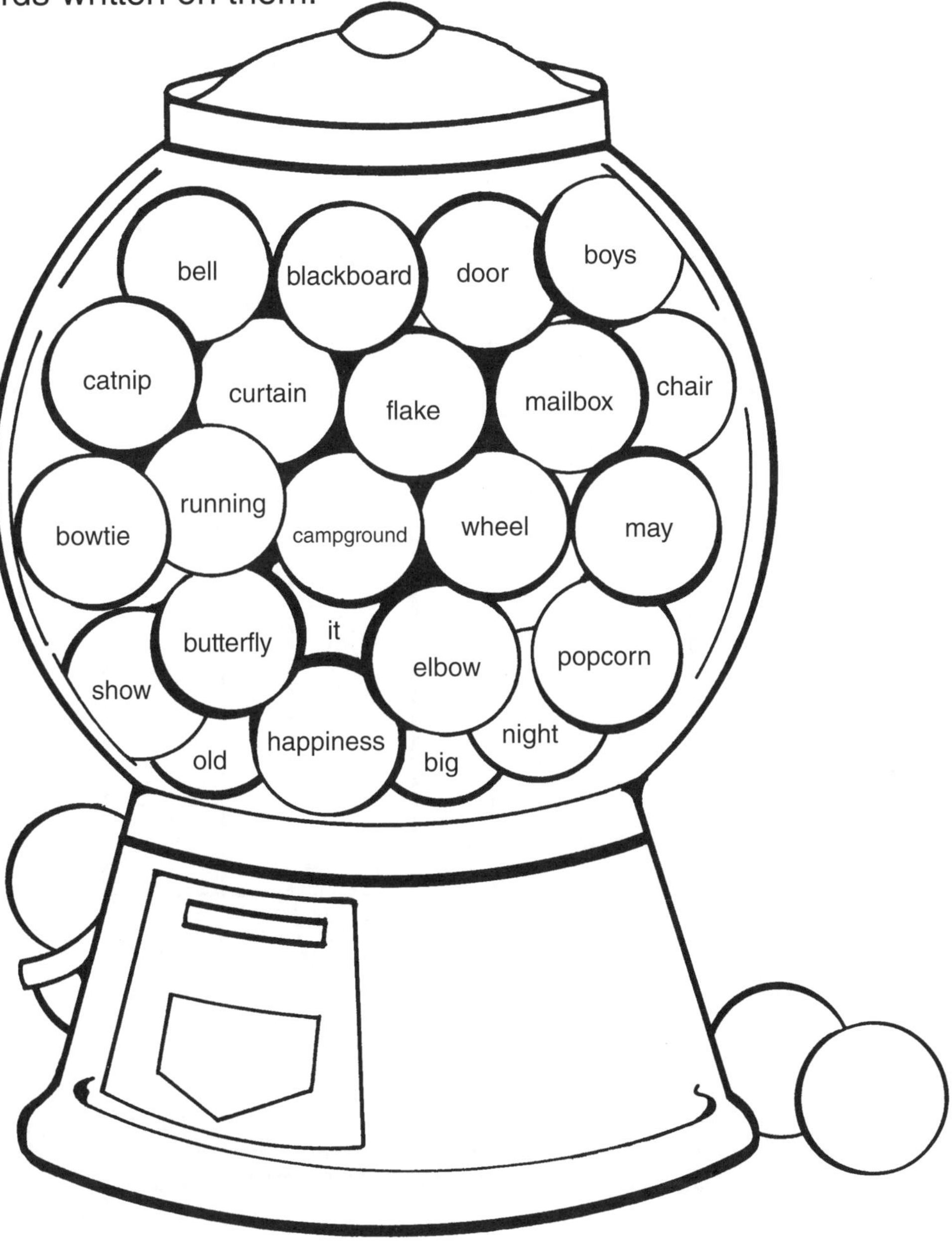

Pipe Organ Addition

Directions: Pipe organs make beautiful music. Each pipe makes a different sound. Add the numbers on the pipes of this organ. Color the pipe with the biggest number.

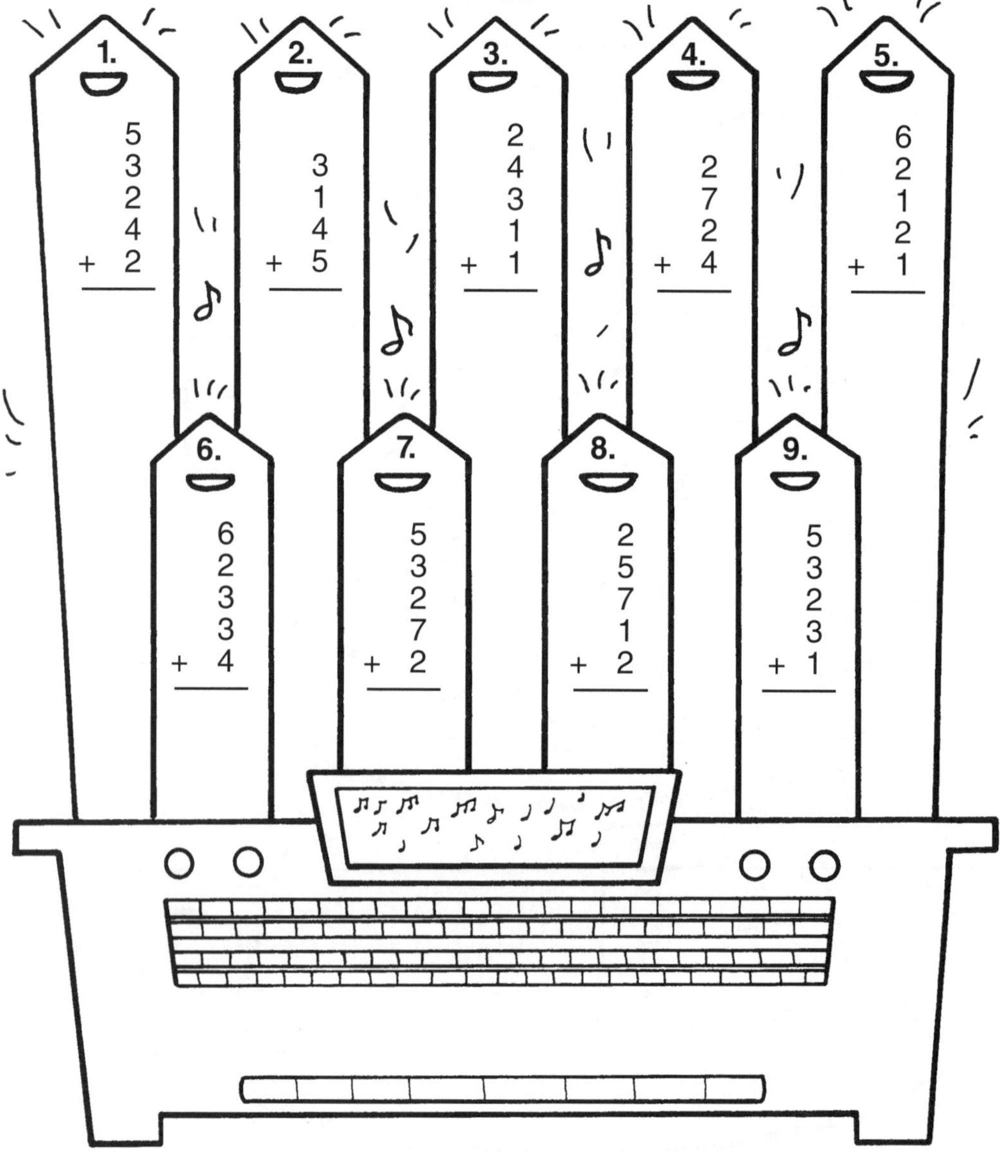

Time to Tell Time

Directions: Match each time below.

1.	seven-thirty	**a.**	9:00
2.	eight-fifteen	**b.**	7:30
3.	nine o'clock	**c.**	12:00
4.	five-fifteen	**d.**	8:15
5.	twelve noon	**e.**	5:15

Directions: Draw the time given on the empty clock face.

6.

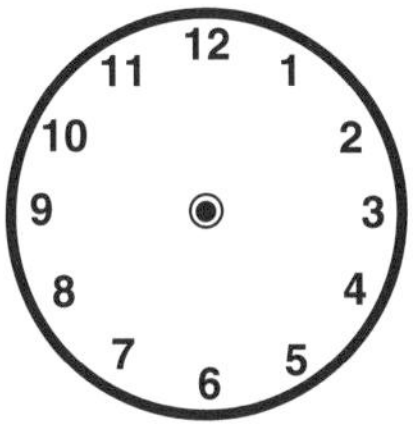

3:15

7.

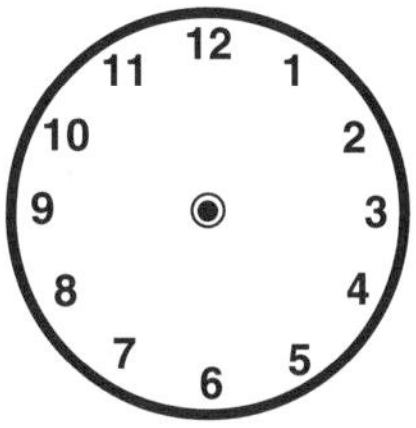

8:00

8.

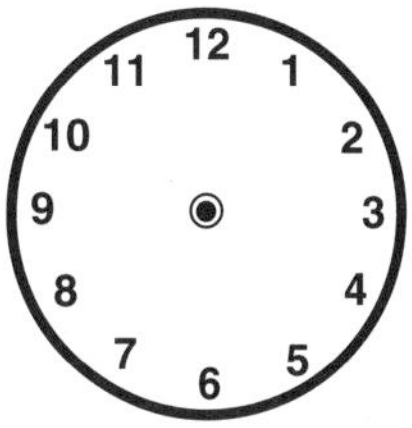

9:30

9.

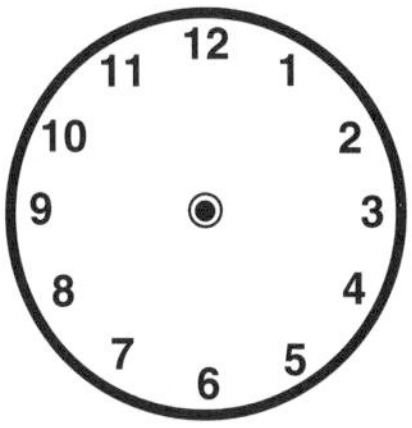

7:15

10.

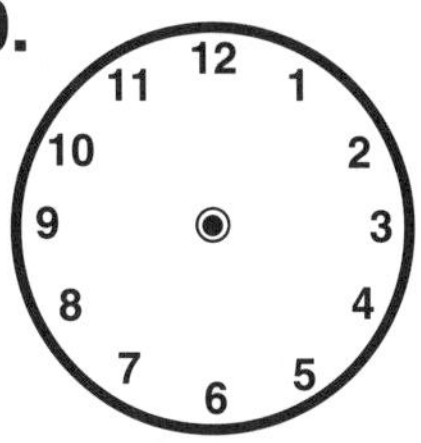

8:30

11.

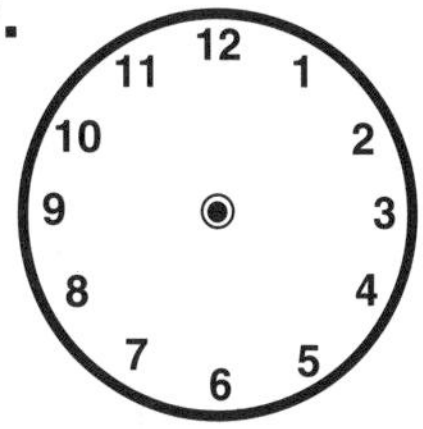

2:00

Fill in the Boxes

Directions: Solve each problem.

1. Write the missing addend.

$$\begin{array}{r} 30 \\ + \ \square \\ \hline 70 \end{array}$$

2. Write the missing addend.

$$\begin{array}{r} 90 \\ + \ \square \\ \hline 90 \end{array}$$

3. Write the missing addend.

$$\begin{array}{r} 20 \\ + \ \square \\ \hline 80 \end{array}$$

4. Complete the table.

+	1	2	3	4	5	6
10						

5. Complete the table.

+	10	20	30	40	50	60
5						

Number Practice

Directions: Follow the instructions in each box.

1. Write the numbers in order from smallest to greatest.

86 15 27 4

______, ______, ______, ______

2. Write the numbers in order from smallest to greatest.

0 92 18 30

______, ______, ______, ______

3. Write the numbers in order from greatest to smallest.

86 15 87 14

______, ______, ______, ______

4. Write each number in standard form.

thirty-eight ______________

sixty-two ______________

forty-five ______________

5. Write each number in standard form.

ninety-one ______________

fifty-six ______________

fifty-eight ______________

A Dozen Eggs

Directions: Look at each egg carton. Count to see how many eggs there are in each one. How many more are needed to make a dozen? Write a subtraction sentence for each carton.

1. 12 – ____ = ________

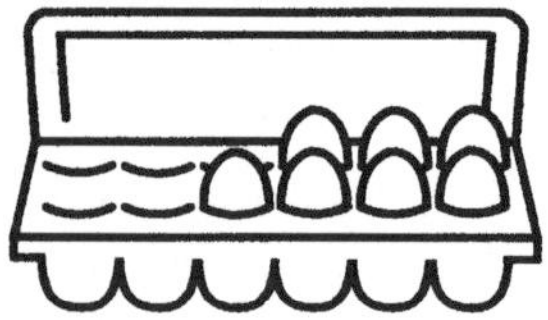

2. 12 – ____ = ________

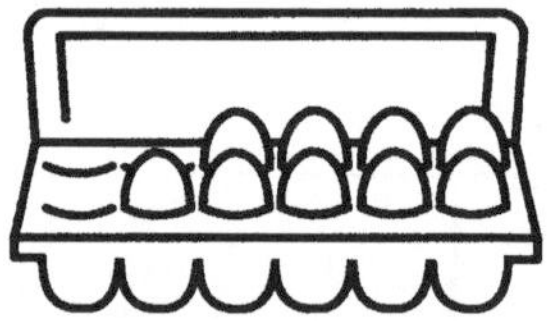

3. 12 – ____ = ________

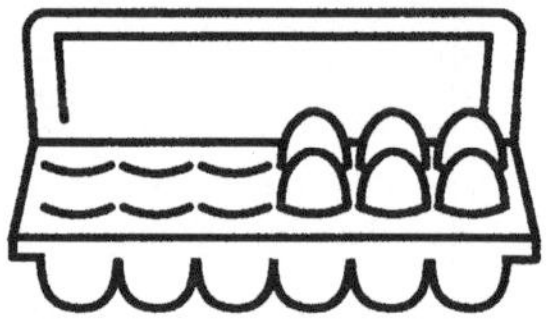

4. 12 – ____ = ________

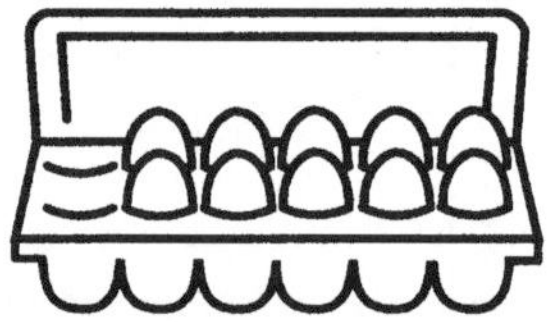

5. 12 – ____ = ________

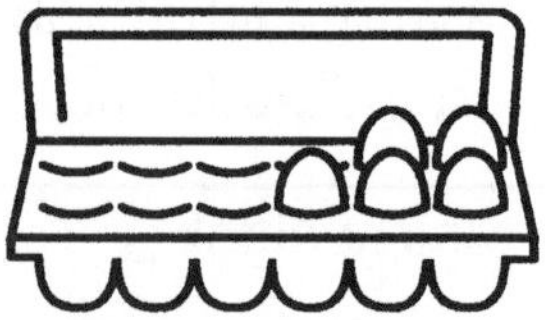

6. 12 – ____ = ________

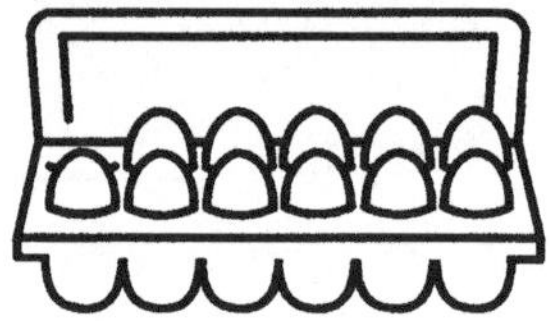

What's the Scoop?

Directions: Fill in the number on each cone to complete the problem.

1.

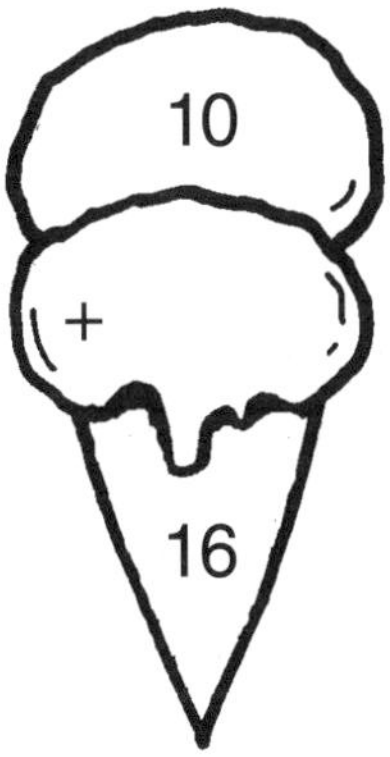

2.

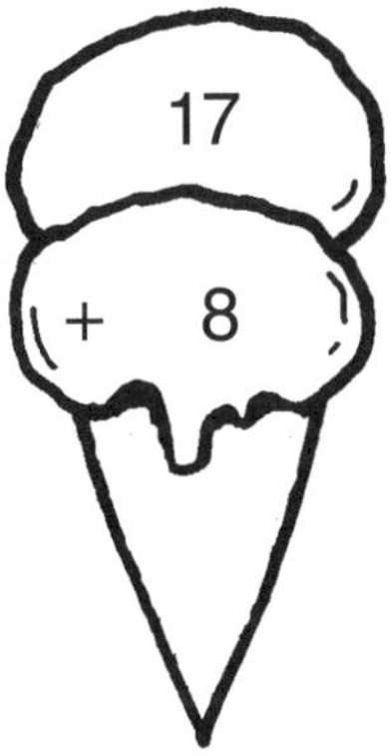

3.

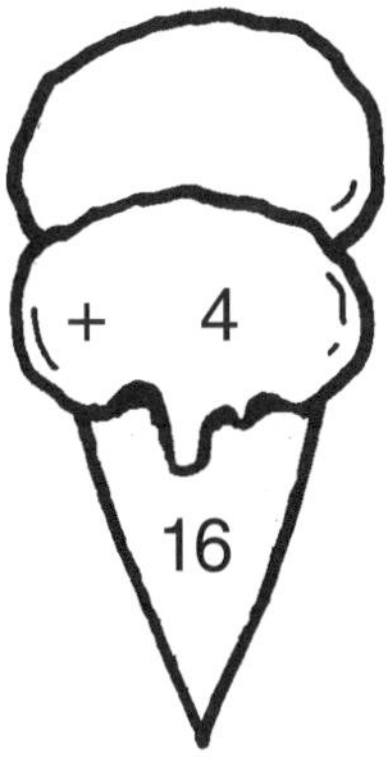

4.

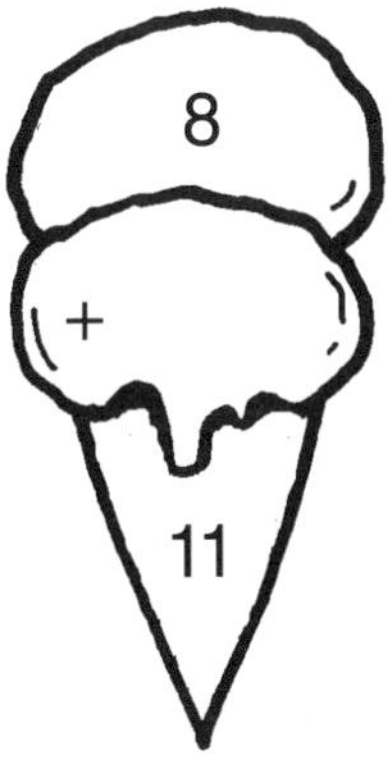

5.

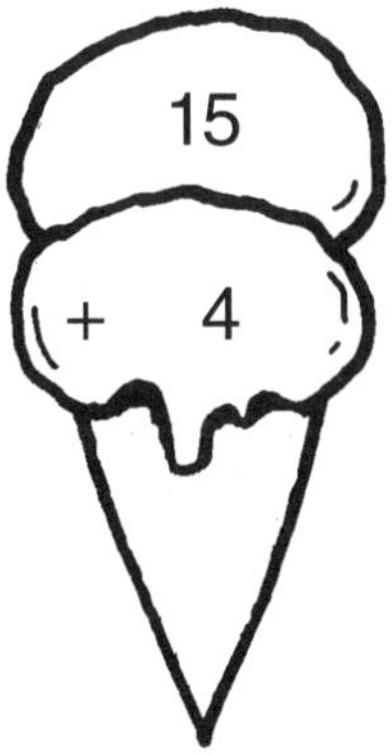

6.

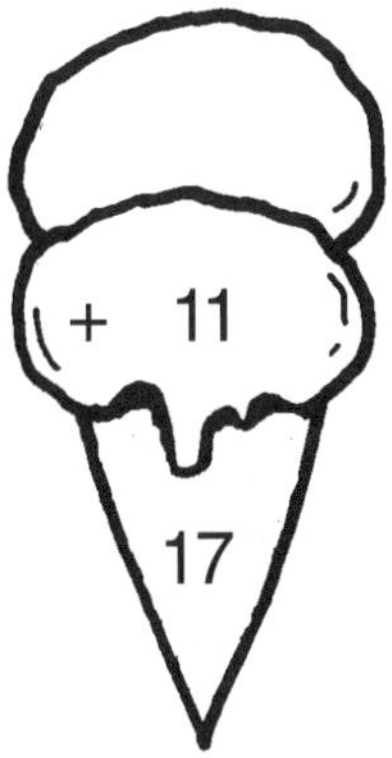

7.

8.

9.

Even Steven

Directions: Even numbers are all whole numbers that can be divided equally in half and remain whole numbers. Color the even numbers.

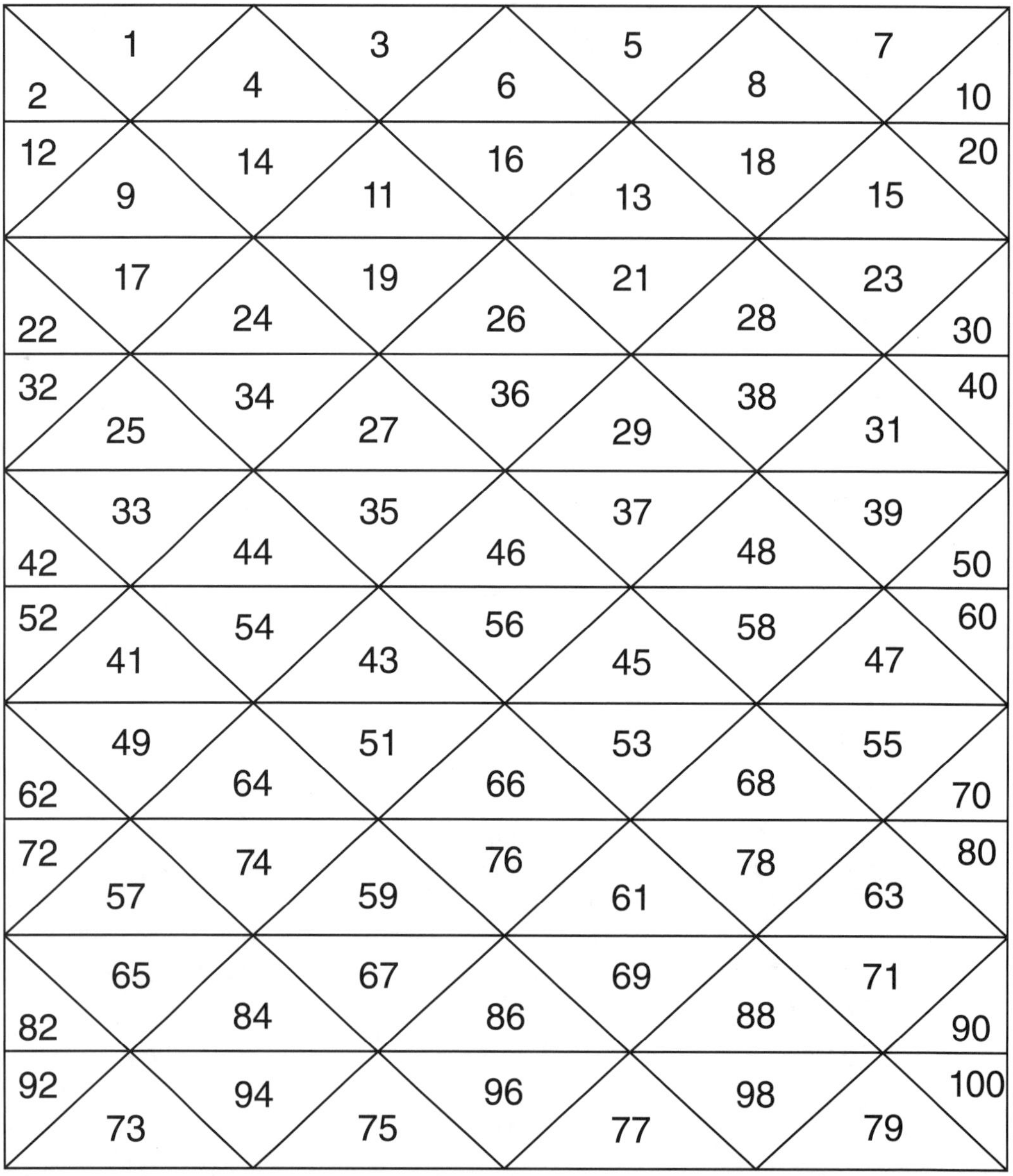

How Odd!

Directions: Odd numbers are all whole numbers that cannot be divided equally in half as whole numbers. Color the odd numbers.

1	2	3	5	4	7	9	6	11
8	13	10	12	15	14	16	17	18
19	20	21	23	22	25	27	24	29
26	31	28	30	33	32	34	35	36
37	38	39	41	40	43	45	42	47
44	49	46	48	51	50	52	53	54
55	56	57	59	58	61	63	60	65
62	67	64	66	69	68	70	71	72
73	74	75	77	76	79	81	78	83
80	85	82	84	87	86	88	89	90
91	92	93	95	94	97	99	96	0

Long, Long Ago

The imprint or remains of something in the earth that lived long, long ago is called a fossil.

Directions: Draw a line and match each fossil to its original source.

1.		**a.** a dragonfly
2.		**b.** a dinosaur
3.		**c.** a fish
4.		**d.** a footprint
5.		**e.** a leaf

Directions: Color the fossils you find.

Predicting Outcomes

Directions: Read the words and look at the pictures. What do you think will happen? Complete the last box with a picture and a sentence.

1. A big wind started to blow.

2. Leaves flew in whirlpools of air.

3. The old tree swayed and bent in the wind.

4.

Ready·Set·Learn

Capitalization

Directions: Put the proper nouns from the word box in their correct columns below. Be sure to add the capital letters!

rocky mountains	plum street	thanksgiving	halloween
mr. peterson	august	fluffy	sandy
november	memorial day	christmas	february
russia	alexander	south america	march

Names *(people and pets)*

____
____
____
____
____

Places

____
____
____
____
____

Months

____
____
____
____
____

Holidays

____
____
____
____
____

This Land Is Your Land

Directions: Read and follow each direction.

1.	2.
Imagine you could name a new country. What would you name it? Draw a picture of the new country. ________________________	Every country has a flag that tells something about the country. Draw and color the new flag. Write one thing that is special about it. ________________________

3.

Many countries have a symbol or statue. For example, the United States has the Statue of Liberty. Draw a symbol for the country. What is the name of your symbol?

____

Compound Practice

Directions: Using the words in the box below, write the compound word for each picture.

1.  ______________________

2.  ______________________

3.  ______________________

4.  ______________________

5.  ______________________

6.  ______________________

board	fire	rattle
camp	flash	scare
chalk	flower	snake
crow	light	sun

Irregular Plurals

Directions: Find the plural forms of these words in the word search. The first one has been done for you.

man	tooth	knife
woman	foot	leaf
mouse	goose	life

A	W	W	M	M	E	N	E	G	G
L	N	O	A	V	H	F	F	S	G
L	Z	B	M	N	T	E	E	T	H
K	E	I	G	E	E	S	E	L	R
M	F	A	M	U	N	T	T	I	E
K	C	T	V	I	M	C	D	V	Q
Y	K	J	M	E	C	P	D	E	I
K	N	I	V	E	S	E	J	S	H

Homophones

Directions: Choose the correct homophone to use in each sentence.

	Sentence		
1.	They collected sea shells in the ________.	**pail**	**pale**
2.	________ friends went to the concert.	**Two**	**To**
3.	Do you ________ that noise?	**here**	**hear**
4.	I am going to ________ my new sweater.	**wear**	**where**
5.	He will have to ________ his button onto his shirt.	**so**	**sew**
6.	The snow fell ________ in the mountains.	**hi**	**high**
7.	Collect some ________ for the fire.	**wood**	**would**
8.	A buzzing ________ flew to the hive.	**be**	**bee**
9.	The wind ________ across the water.	**blew**	**blue**
10.	I ________ you would come!	**knew**	**new**

Analogies

Directions: Analogies are comparisons. Complete each analogy below. An example has been done for you.

***Nephew* is to *uncle* as *niece* is to *aunt*.**

1. *See* is to *eye* as ____________ is to *nose*.

2. *Ping-Pong*® is to *paddle* as ____________ is to *racquet*.

3. *Writer* is to *story* as *poet* is to ____________ .

4. *Car* is to ____________ as *plane* is to *pilot*.

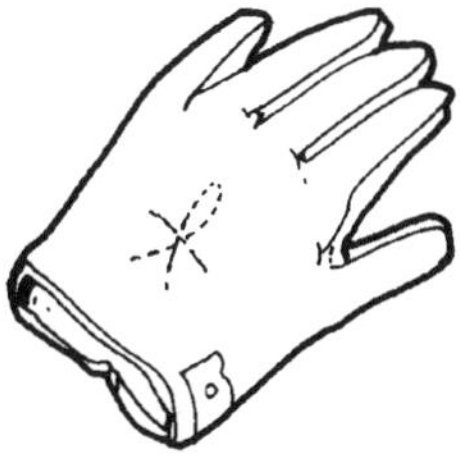

5. *Glove* is to *hand* as *sock* is to ____________ .

6. *Paintbrush* is to ___________________ as *pen* is to *writer*.

7. *Ant* is to __________________ as *bee* is to *hive*.

8. *Sing* is to *song* as __________________ is to *book*.

9. *Left* is to ____________ as *top* is to *bottom*.

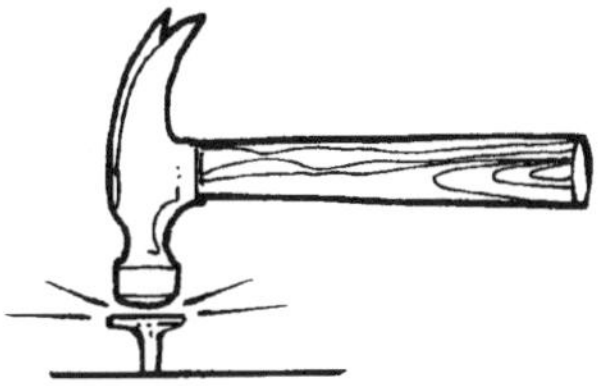

10. ____________ is to *pool* as *jog* is to *road*.

11. *Wrist* is to *hand* as ____________ is to *foot*.

12. *Hammer* is to *nail* as ___________________ is to *screw*.

How Long?

Directions: Look at each event and circle which time measurement you would use to tell how long ago each event happened. Use the information in the box to help you.

one year = 365 days = **Y**
one decade = 10 years = **D**
one century = 100 years or 10 decades = **C**

1. your birth	**Y**	**D**	**C**
2. when dinosaurs lived	**Y**	**D**	**C**
3. your grandparents' births	**Y**	**D**	**C**
4. the Ice Age	**Y**	**D**	**C**
5. the 1950s	**Y**	**D**	**C**
6. the Pilgrims' landing at Plymouth	**Y**	**D**	**C**
7. your second birthday	**Y**	**D**	**C**
8. your first doctor's appointment	**Y**	**D**	**C**
9. your parents' first day at school	**Y**	**D**	**C**
10. your first day at school	**Y**	**D**	**C**

Picture the Story

Directions: Under each picture write a sentence that tells the main idea of what is happening. Color the pictures.

1.

2.

3.

4.

Adjectives

Directions: Which word in the sentence is an adjective? Fill in the bubble next to the word that is the adjective in each sentence.

1. The zebra ate the leaves off of the broken tree.

○ a. zebra ○ b. leaves ○ c. broken ○ d. tree

2. Sven typed on his new computer.

○ a. Sven ○ b. new ○ c. computer ○ d. typed

3. The busy students studied for their tests.

○ a. busy ○ b. students ○ c. tests ○ d. studied

4. A curious bug scurried under the rug.

○ a. rug ○ b. scurried ○ c. bug ○ d. curious

5. Steve and Tom ate all of the cheese pizza.

○ a. Steve ○ b. pizza ○ c. cheese ○ d. ate

6. The boys painted their names on the beautiful mural.

○ a. boys ○ b. painted ○ c. beautiful ○ d. mural

7. I stared at my cold spaghetti.

○ a. cold ○ b. ate ○ c. spaghetti ○ d. stared

Fruits

Directions: Use the clues below to fill in the puzzle with the names of fruits.

Across

3. green or purple; wine is made from them

6. yellow and sour

8. same as its color; make juice from it

9. small and red

10. yellow or orange; usually is more tart than sweet

Down

1. give it to your teacher

2. sweet; red; with a green stem on top

4. large; green on the outside and red with many pits on the inside; very sweet

5. grows in a palm tree; very hard shell

7. yellow and long

Triple the Fun

Directions: Add the three digit numbers to find the answer.

1. 309 + 208	**2.** 128 + 222	**3.** 672 + 109
4. 111 + 119	**5.** 775 + 127	**6.** 222 + 219
7. 543 + 318	**8.** 345 + 425	**9.** 467 + 314

The Balloon Clown

Directions: Solve the problems on the balloons. Use the code to color each balloon.

54 = yellow	75 = blue	52 = green	45 = pink
88 = orange	36 = red	63 = purple	96 = brown

1. $\begin{array}{r} 49 \\ +\ 39 \\ \hline \end{array}$

2. $\begin{array}{r} 57 \\ +\ 18 \\ \hline \end{array}$

3. $\begin{array}{r} 18 \\ +\ 18 \\ \hline \end{array}$

4. $\begin{array}{r} 38 \\ +\ 58 \\ \hline \end{array}$

5. $\begin{array}{r} 16 \\ +\ 36 \\ \hline \end{array}$

6. $\begin{array}{r} 47 \\ +\ 16 \\ \hline \end{array}$

7. $\begin{array}{r} 27 \\ +\ 27 \\ \hline \end{array}$

8. $\begin{array}{r} 27 \\ +\ 18 \\ \hline \end{array}$

Right on Target

Directions: Solve each subtraction problem to hit the center of the target.

1. $754 - 135$

2. $888 - 777$

3. $721 - 432$

4. $312 - 289$

5. $211 - 101$

6. $621 - 403$

7. $110 - 100$

8. $389 - 299$

9. $489 - 150$

10. $923 - 554$

11. $117 - 117$

12. $827 - 236$

The Decimal Horse Race

Directions: And they're off! There's No Chance in the outside lane, Fat Chance in the middle lane, and Slim Chance in the inside lane. Who will win the derby? Add each number each horse crosses. The horse with the *lowest* total at the end wins!

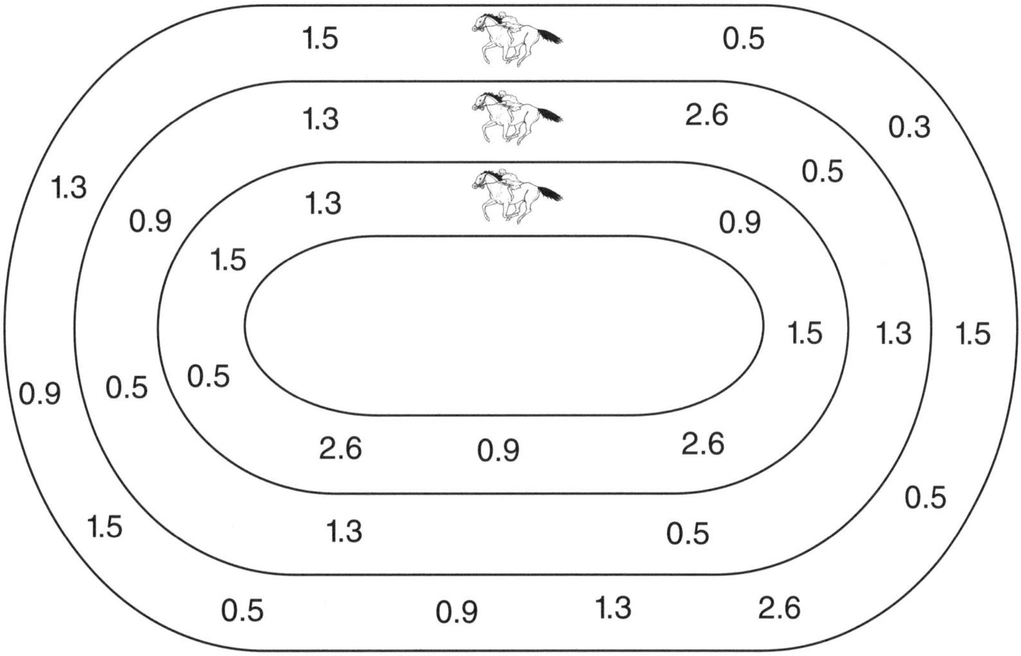

Final Count

No Chance _____ Fat Chance _____ Slim Chance _____

Who won? ______________________________

Finding Patterns

Directions: Finding patterns is like solving puzzles. See if you can match the patterns below. Draw a line from each pattern on the left to its partner on the right.

1. up, down, up

2. 10, 20, 30

3. blue, red, red

4. 9, 18, 27

5. 20, 19, 18

6. Z, Y, X

7. January, February, March

8. boy, girl, boy

9. 800, 700, 600

10. !, ?, !

a. 40, 50, 60

b. W, V, U

c. April, May, June

d. ?, !, ?

e. girl, boy, girl

f. 500, 400, 300

g. 17, 16, 15

h. blue, red, red

i. 36, 45, 54

j. down, up, down

Directions: Complete each pattern.

11. 10 x 10, 11 x 11, 12 x 12, __________, __________, __________

12. ABC, DEF, GHI, __________, __________, __________

13. 1, 22, 333, __________, __________, __________

14. 25, 40, 55, __________, __________, __________

15. 1/4, 1/5, 1/6, __________, __________, __________

Subtraction Solutions

Directions: Fill in the puzzle by solving the subtraction problems. Use the number names in the Word List.

Word List				
eleven	thirteen	fifteen	seventeen	nineteen
twelve	fourteen	sixteen	eighteen	twenty

Across

1. 25 – 11 =
3. 40 – 21 =
7. 33 – 16 =
9. 51 – 35 =

Down

1. 46 – 31 =
2. 27 – 7 =
4. 22 – 4 =
5. 19 – 8 =
6. 44 – 32 =
8. 38 – 25 =

Dividing and Multiplying Go Together

Directions: Complete each set of related problems.

1. 27 ÷ 3 = __________ 3 x 9 = __________

2. 12 ÷ 4 = __________ 4 x 3 = __________

3. 18 ÷ 6 = __________ 6 x 3 = __________

4. 10 ÷ 2 = __________ 2 x 5 = __________

5. 88 ÷ 11 =__________ 11 x 8 = __________

6. 45 ÷ 9 = __________ 9 x 5 = __________

7. 7 ÷ 1 = __________ 1 x 7 = __________

8. 28 ÷ 4 = __________ 4 x 7 = __________

9. 36 ÷ 3 = __________ 3 x 12 = __________

10. 60 ÷ 10 = __________ 10 x 6 = __________

11. 44 ÷ 4 = __________ 4 x 11 = __________

12. 24 ÷ 6 = __________ 6 x 4 = __________

13. 50 ÷ 5 = __________ 5 x 10 = __________

14. 56 ÷ 8 = __________ 8 x 7 = __________

15. 14 ÷ 2 = __________ 2 x 7 = __________

Patterns in Division

Directions: You can do long division problems quickly if you understand the pattern. Find the pattern for each set of division problems. Then divide to find the answers.

1.	$2\overline{)4}$	$2\overline{)40}$	$2\overline{)400}$	$2\overline{)4{,}000}$
2.	$2\overline{)6}$	$2\overline{)60}$	$2\overline{)600}$	$2\overline{)6{,}000}$
3.	$7\overline{)28}$	$7\overline{)280}$	$7\overline{)2{,}800}$	$7\overline{)28{,}000}$
4.	$1\overline{)6}$	$1\overline{)60}$	$1\overline{)600}$	$1\overline{)6{,}000}$
5.	$4\overline{)20}$	$4\overline{)200}$	$4\overline{)2{,}000}$	$4\overline{)20{,}000}$
6.	$3\overline{)9}$	$3\overline{)90}$	$3\overline{)900}$	$3\overline{)9{,}000}$
7.	$5\overline{)5}$	$5\overline{)50}$	$5\overline{)500}$	$5\overline{)5{,}000}$
8.	$8\overline{)32}$	$8\overline{)320}$	$8\overline{)3{,}200}$	$8\overline{)32{,}000}$

Flowering Factors

Directions: Color the factors for 12 red and the remaining numbers green.

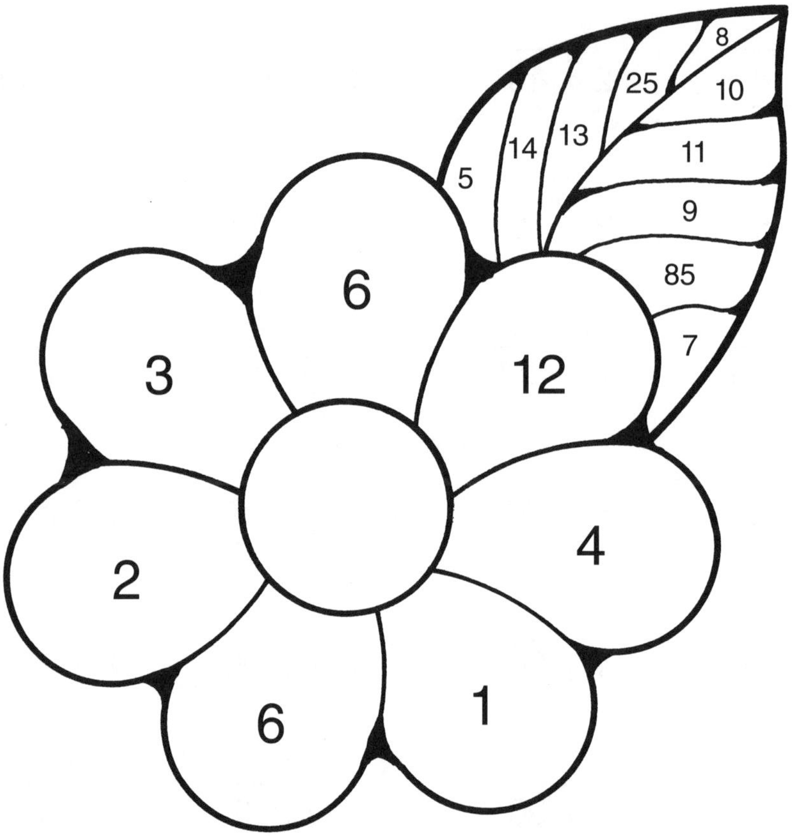

Circle the factors for 16.

3	4	9	7
5	6	8	2

Circle the factors for 20.

10	2	8	9
3	7	5	4

Sentence Detective

Directions: There are only 10 complete sentences shown in the magnifying glass. Circle these 10 sentences.

I'm going swimming after school!
Tuesday.
Chris opens the door.
April.
Will we go to the store tomorrow?
paper bag?
My iguana ate my homework.
Juanita helps me.
Can you come with me?
the lights!
My best friend?
Maria dances every day.
I have a cat.
That bicycle looks brand new!
Do you like candy?

Which Is It?

Directions: Circle the word or number that correctly corresponds.

1. Pentagon	2 sides	5 sides	7 sides
2. Hawaii	island	peninsula	lake
3. State	Oregon	Africa	Sacramento
4. Abraham Lincoln	16th president	2nd president	38th president
5. Painter	Shakespeare	Mozart	Rembrandt
6. Baby kangaroo	billy	bobby	joey
7. Leap year	11 months	49 weeks	366 days
8. String instrument	saxophone	violin	drums
9. Continents on Earth	5	7	9
10. French city	London	Paris	Rome

What Doesn't Belong?

Directions: One of the four words in each group below does not belong with the other three. Circle the one that does not fit. Then, explain what the others have in common. An example has been done for you.

Australia, South America, Europe, (France) They are continents.

1. pen, pencil, chalk, eraser ______________________
2. violin, horn, cello, guitar ______________________
3. milk, half & half, cream, eggs ______________________
4. cedar, oak, pearl, walnut ______________________
5. penny, dollar bill, quarter, dime ______________________
6. jet, helicopter, rocket, ship ______________________
7. pretty, alarmed, afraid, frightened ______________________
8. ample, lots, few, plenty ______________________
9. screwdriver, hammer, drawer, saw ______________________
10. lime, lemon, apple, orange ______________________

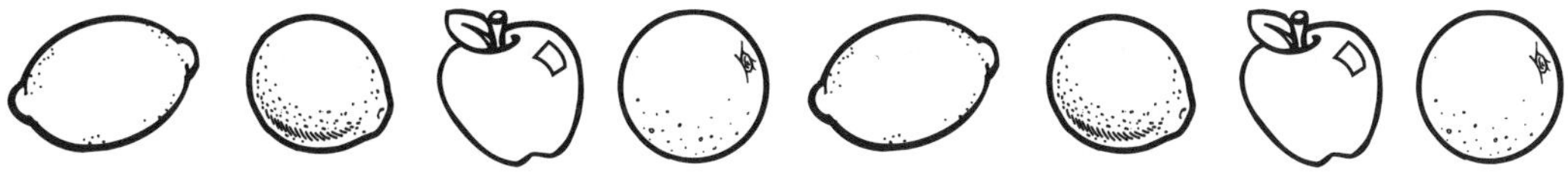

School Supplies

Directions: Use the chart to answer each question below.

School Store

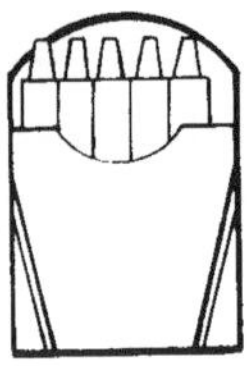
36¢

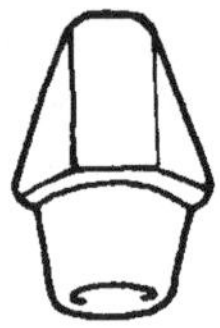
18¢

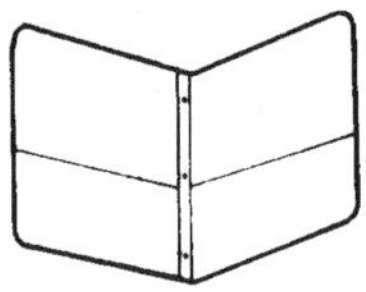
25¢

22¢

40¢

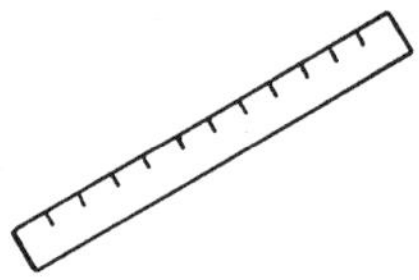
20¢

1. Jane has 85¢. She buys a pencil. Jane will have ________ left over.

2. Ryan has 75¢. He buys a ruler. Ryan will have ________ left over.

3. Danielle has 59¢. She buys an eraser. Danielle will have ________ left over.

4. Gregory has 35¢. He buys a folder. Gregory will have ________ left over.

5. Lorenzo has 97¢. He buys glue and a pencil. Lorenzo will have ________ left over.

Magical Multiplication

Directions: Multiply going across and down. Write the missing numbers. Study the example.

Example

x →

5	5	25
6	2	12
30	10	300

Square #1

x →

2		14
	5	
12		420

Square #2

x →

10		20
	6	
40		480

Square #3

x →

6		6
	3	
66		198

Past, Present, and Future

Directions: Look at each invention or possible invention. Decide if it is an invention that was used in the past, an invention that is used in the present, or an invention that might be used in the future. Circle your answer.

1.  a spinning wheel — **past** **present** **future**

2.  satellite television — **past** **present** **future**

3.  cars that fly in the air — **past** **present** **future**

4.  telephones with caller identification — **past** **present** **future**

5. 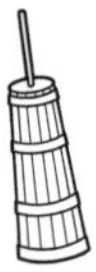 a butter churn — **past** **present** **future**

6.  cellular phones — **past** **present** **future**

7.  robots working as maids in every home — **past** **present** **future**

8.  notebook computers — **past** **present** **future**

Color Code

Directors: Make your own color chart for this picture. Then color the picture in the colors you chose for the chart.

number	color to use
1	
2	
3	
4	
5	
6	
7	

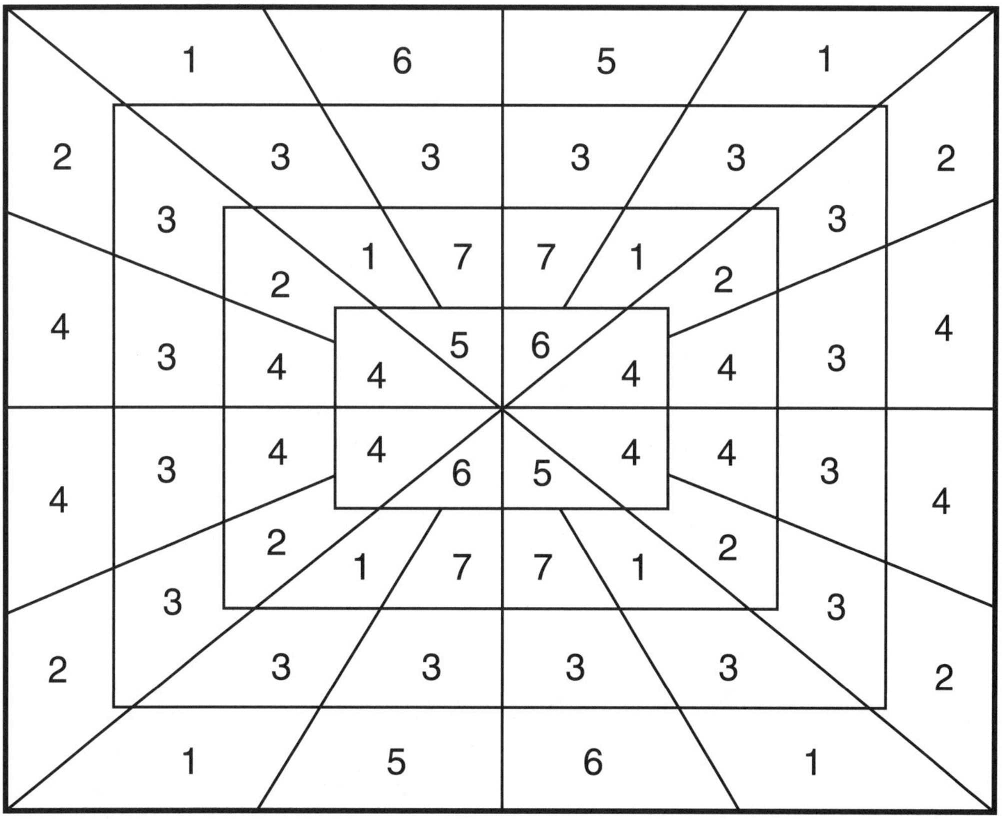

Farm Punctuation

Directions: Read the story below. Add the missing punctuation.

Have you ever been on a farm

Mrs Young took her third grade class to Mr Frank s farm on Tuesday morning They saw cows chickens and horses Mr Frank wanted to know if any students would like to ride a horse Leslie screamed I do John and Carl wanted to ride too Mrs Young s class will never forget the special day on the farm

Rhymes

Directions: Rhyming words have the same end sounds, but those end sounds are not always spelled in the same way. Match the rhyming pairs by coloring each matching pair the same color.

1.	alone	wrote
2.	bowl	bale
3.	coat	bees
4.	home	fly
5.	mail	frayed
6.	maid	great
7.	plate	known
8.	seize	roam
9.	sigh	roll
10.	soap	rope

Silent E

Directions: Sometimes the letter *e* in a word has no sound, but its job is still important. It changes a short vowel sound to a long one. Read the words below. Then write the word on the blank, adding an *e*. Read the new words.

1. can **2.** sit **3.** cap

4. tub

5. dot

6. not

7. rat

8. lob **9.** bit

10. cub

11. grim

12. fin

13. bath **14.** van **15.** plan

1. ______________________

2. ______________________

3. ______________________

4. ______________________

5. ______________________

6. ______________________

7. ______________________

8. ______________________

9. ______________________

10. ______________________

11. ______________________

12. ______________________

13. ______________________

14. ______________________

15. ______________________

Consonant

Directions: List all the words you can think of that begin with the following consonant blends.

bl	br	cl

dr	fl	fr

gr	pl	str

Draw the Dots

Directions: Solve each problem by drawing dots or lines to represent each number. Add to find the sum. Circle the correct answer.

Example: 15 + 11 =

(A.) 26
B. 30
C. 4
D. 27

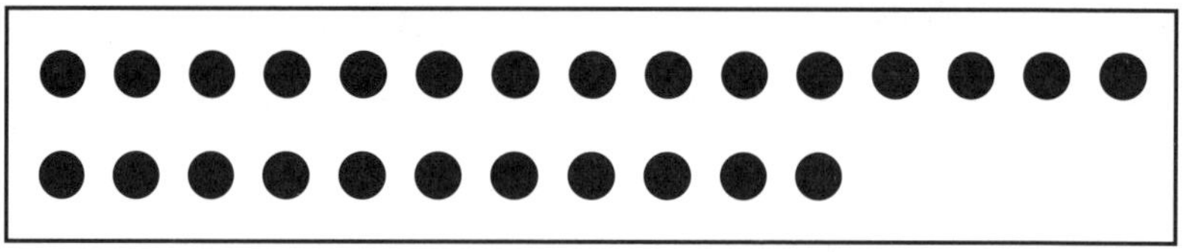

1. 18 + 9 =

A. 23
B. 26
C. 9
D. 27

2. 12 + 12 =

A. 24
B. 12
C. 26
D. 0

3. 6 + 9 =

A. 17
B. 15
C. 3
D. 16

4. 20 + 8 =

A. 30
B. 18
C. 12
D. 28

A Part of the Group

Directions: Look at each group and write a fraction for the answer.

Example: How many of the stars have stripes? $\frac{3}{5}$ have stripes.

1. What fraction of the circles have polka dots?

____

2. What fraction of the diamonds are shaded in?

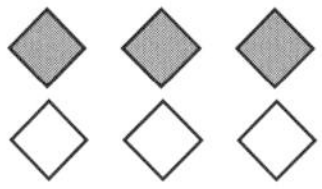

____

3. What fraction of the triangles are shaded in?

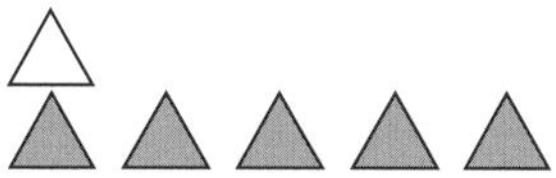

____

4. What fraction of the squares have stripes?

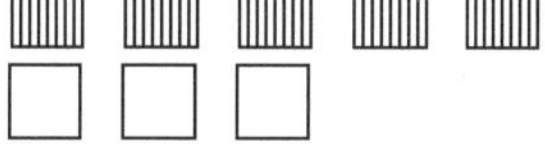

____

5. What fraction of the circles have smiley faces?

____

6. What fraction of the squares are shaded in?

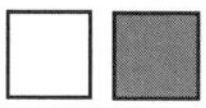

____

Favorite Holiday

What is your favorite holiday? ______________________________

After deciding, write a paragraph about your favorite holiday.

Beginning: In a complete sentence, tell which holiday is your favorite.

____

____

Middle: In several complete sentences, tell why it is your favorite and how you and your family celebrate it.

____

____

____

____

____

Ending: Tell the name of the holiday again and repeat why it is your favorite.

____

____

Geography Search

O	C	E	N	C	O	N	T	I	N	O	N	T	S	E	A
A	N	T	A	R	C	T	I	C	A	N	C	E	A	E	C
N	S	E	E	R	E	M	A	M	I	C	R	A	E	U	I
T	R	I	S	T	A	S	S	A	D	R	M	T	M	R	R
I	C	C	A	O	M	B	L	U	N	E	Y	L	A	O	E
C	B	I	N	P	A	C	I	F	I	C	A	A	E	P	M
M	E	D	I	T	E	R	R	A	N	E	A	N	S	E	A
A	R	S	H	N	M	N	M	N	N	A	R	T	K	K	H
E	I	A	C	K	C	A	L	P	U	S	R	I	C	A	T
S	N	P	H	L	A	R	C	T	I	C	E	C	A	S	R
D	G	O	T	B	A	C	K	I	M	R	A	A	L	E	O
E	S	O	U	T	H	A	M	E	R	I	C	A	B	A	N
R	E	T	O	O	C	I	X	E	M	F	O	F	L	U	G
M	A	U	S	T	R	A	L	I	A	P	A	T	O	T	O

OCEANS	***CONTINENTS***	***SEAS***
ARCTIC	AFRICA	ARABIAN SEA
ATLANTIC	ANTARCTICA	BERING SEA
INDIAN	ASIA	BLACK SEA
PACIFIC	AUSTRALIA	GULF OF MEXICO
	EUROPE	MEDITERRANEAN SEA
	NORTH AMERICA	RED SEA
	SOUTH AMERICA	SOUTH CHINA SEA

What Time Is It?

Directions: Read the time on the clocks. Write the time on the lines.

1.

____

2.

____

3.

____

4.

____

5.

____

6.

____

7.

____

8.

____

9.

____

A.M. and P.M.

Directions: Write "A.M." or "P.M." after each of these events to say what time of day it usually falls in.

1. dinnertime ______________________

2. getting up ______________________

3. afternoon nap ______________________

4. after-school baseball game ______________________

5. before-school dance class ______________________

6. breakfast ______________________

7. evening movie ______________________

8. evening bath ______________________

9. after-dinner dessert ______________________

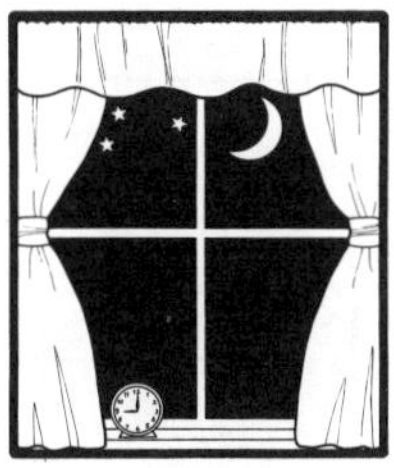

10. sunrise ______________________

11. going to school ______________________

12. sunset ______________________

Ready·Set·Learn

In Your Places!

Directions: First, decode the key by solving some simple number problems. Then, replace each icon with the correct digit and write the number it represents on the line to the right.

Key

Clue	Icon	Number
Number of cents in a nickel		
Number of horns on a unicorn		
Number of sides on a stop sign		
Number of wheels on a bicycle		
Number of leaves on a lucky clover		
Number of dwarves in *Snow White*		

	thousands	hundreds	tens	ones	
1.					24
2.					
3.					
4.					
5.					
6.					

Picture Fractions

Directions: Write the fraction represented by the shaded portion of each picture.

1. 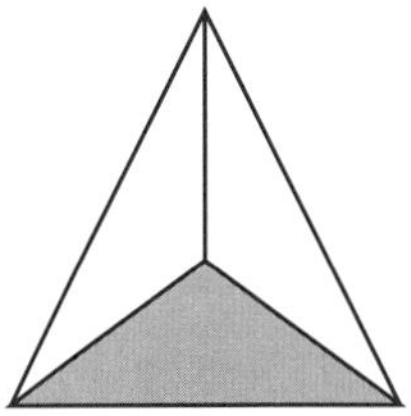 ____________

5. 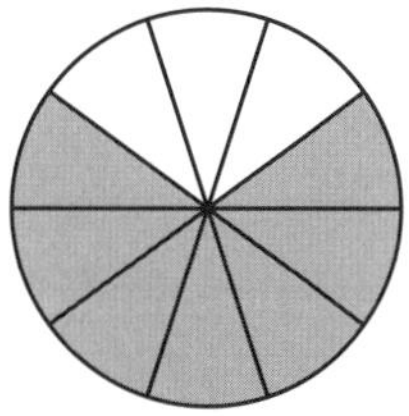 ____________

2. 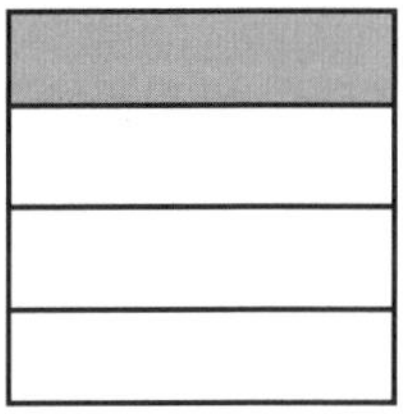 ____________

6. 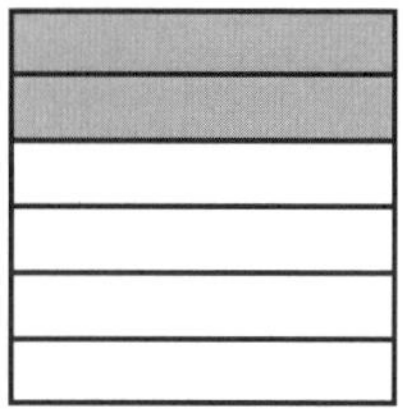 ____________

3. 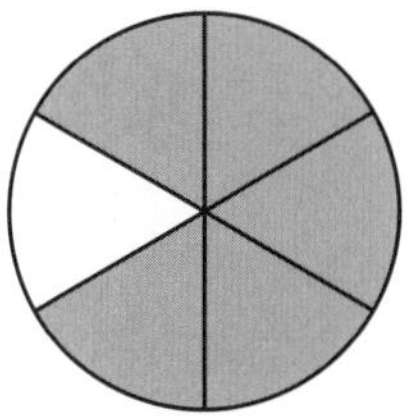 ____________

7. 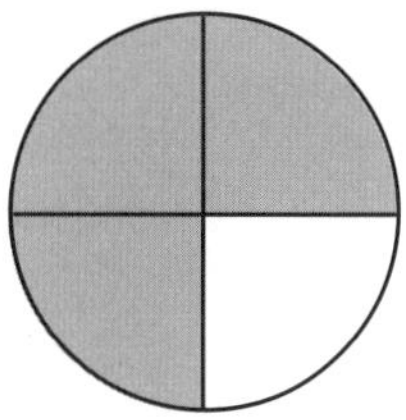 ____________

4. 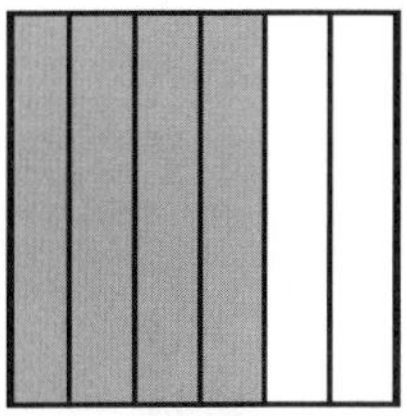 ____________

8. 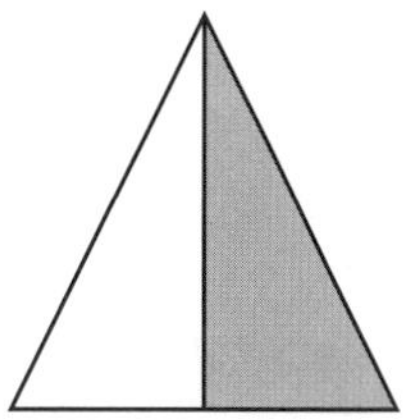 ____________

Your Name

Directions: Write all of the letters of your first and last name. How many words of three or more letters can you make from your name? Write those words inside the alphabet frame.

Your Name: ______________________________________

Answer Key

Page 5

Baseball: bat, centerfield, mitt, shortstop, World Series

Football: face mask, goal posts, Super Bowl, touchdown, helmet

Soccer: goalie, penalty kick, shin guards, yellow card, World Cup

Tennis: ace, court, racquet, serve, Wimbledon

Page 6

1. +   7. x
2. ÷   8. ÷
3. +   9. –
4. –   10. +
5. +   11. x
6. x   12. +

Page 7

1.

11	6	7
4	8	12
9	10	5

2.

5	4	9
10	6	2
3	8	7

3.

6	7	2
1	5	9
8	3	4

Page 8

Pairs: circle/ring, dawn/morning, happy/gleeful, clean/spotless, cloth/fabric, sick/ill, sunny/bright, laugh/chuckle.

Page 9

1. sad   9. empty
2. afraid   10. frown
3. wrong   11. far
4. slow   12. quiet
5. little   13. answer
6. polite   14. tame
7. young   15. ugly
8. weak   16. easy

Page 10

1. bat   6. keep
2. rain   7. ten
3. wake   8. yell
4. say   9. tent
5. peel   10. ring

Page 11

Colored: blackboard, catnip, mailbox, bowtie, campground, butterfly, popcorn.

Page 12

1. 16   6. 18
2. 13   7. 19
3. 11   8. 17
4. 15   9. 14
5. 12

Page 13

1. b   4. e
2. d   5. c
3. a

Page 14

1. 40
2. 0
3. 60
4. 11, 12, 13, 14, 15, 16
5. 15, 25, 35, 45, 55, 65

Page 15

1. 4, 15, 27, 86
2. 0, 18, 30, 92
3. 87, 86, 15, 14
4. 38, 62, 45
5. 91, 56, 58

Page 16

1. 12 – 5 = 7   4. 12 – 2 = 10
2. 12 – 3 = 9   5. 12 – 7 = 5
3. 12 – 6 = 6   6. 12 – 1 = 11

Page 17

1. 6   6. 6
2. 25   7. 9
3. 12   8. 21
4. 3   9. 7
5. 19

Page 20

1. e   4. b
2. a   5. c
3. d

Page 22

Names: Mr. Peterson, Alexander, Fluffy, Sandy

Places: Rocky Mountains, Russia, Plum Street, South America

Months: November, August, February, March

Holidays: Memorial Day, Thanksgiving, Christmas, Halloween

Page 24

1. chalkboard   4. campfire
2. flashlight   5. scarecrow
3. sunflower   6. rattlesnake

Page 25

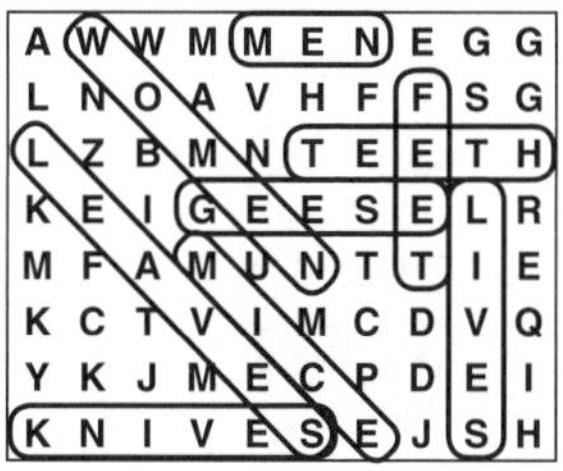

Page 26

1. pail   6. high
2. Two   7. wood
3. hear   8. bee
4. wear   9. blew
5. sew   10. knew

Page 27

1. smell   7. hill
2. tennis   8. read
3. poem   9. right
4. driver   10. swim
5. foot   11. ankle
6. painter   12. screwdriver

Page 28

1. years   6. centuries
2. centuries   7. years
3. decades   8. years
4. centuries   9. decades
5. decades   10. years

Page 30

1. c   5. c
2. b   6. c
3. a   7. a
4. d

Page 31

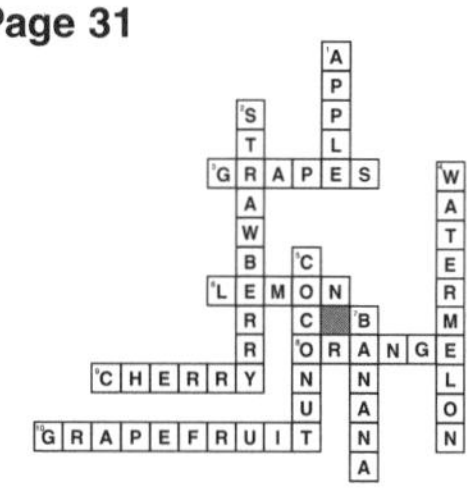

Page 32

1. 517   6. 441
2. 350   7. 861
3. 781   8. 770
4. 230   9. 781
5. 902

Page 33

1. 88   5. 52
2. 75   6. 63
3. 36   7. 54
4. 96   8. 45

Page 34

1. 619   7. 10
2. 111   8. 90
3. 289   9. 339
4. 23   10. 369
5. 110   11. 0
6. 218   12. 591

Page 35

No Chance: 13.3

Fat Chance: 8.9

Slim Chance: 11.8

Fat Chance is the winner.

Answer Key *(cont.)*

Page 36

1. j
2. a
3. h
4. i
5. g
6. b
7. c
8. e
9. f
10. d
11. 13 x 13, 14 x 14, 15 x 15
12. JKL, MNO, PQR
13. 4444, 55555, 666666
14. 70, 85, 100
15. 1/7, 1/8, 1/9

Page 37

Across

1. fourteen
3. nineteen
7. seventeen
9. sixteen

Down

1. fifteen
2. twenty
4. eighteen
5. eleven
6. twelve
8. thirteen

Page 38

1. 9, 27
2. 3, 12
3. 3, 18
4. 5, 10
5. 8, 88
6. 5, 45
7. 7, 7
8. 7, 28
9. 12, 36
10. 6, 60
11. 11, 44
12. 4, 24
13. 10, 50
14. 7, 56
15. 7, 14

Page 39

1. 2; 20; 200; 2,000
2. 3; 30; 300; 3,000
3. 4; 40; 400; 4,000
4. 6; 60; 600; 6,000
5. 5; 50; 500; 5,000
6. 3; 30; 300; 3,000
7. 1; 10; 100; 1,000
8. 4; 40; 400; 4,000

Page 40

Factors for 16: 4, 8, 2
Factors for 20: 10, 2, 5, 4

Page 41

Complete sentences:
I'm going swimming after school!
Chris opens the door.
Will we go to the store tomorrow?
My iguana ate my homework.
Juanita helps me.
Can you come with me?
Maria dances every day.
I have a cat.
That bicycle looks brand new!
Do you like candy?

Page 42

1. 5 sides
2. island
3. Oregon
4. 16th president
5. Rembrandt
6. joey
7. 366 days
8. violin
9. 7
10. Paris

Page 43

1. eraser; writing tools
2. horn; stringed instruments
3. eggs; dairy products
4. pearl; woods
5. dollar bill; coins
6. ship; air transportation
7. pretty; words meaning "scared"
8. few; words meaning "many"
9. drawer; tools
10. apple; citrus fruits

Page 44

1. 63¢
2. 55¢
3. 41¢
4. 10¢
5. 35¢

Page 45

Square #1: (top row) 7; (middle row) 6, 30; (bottom row) 35
Square #2: (top row) 2; (middle row) 4, 24; (bottom row) 12
Square #3: (top row) 1; (middle row) 11, 33; (bottom row) 3

Page 46

1. past
2. present
3. future
4. present
5. past
6. present
7. future
8. present

Page 48

Have you ever been on a farm? Mrs. Young took her third grade class to Mr. Frank's farm on Tuesday morning. They saw cows, chickens, and horses. Mr. Frank wanted to know if any students would like to ride a horse. Leslie screamed, "I do!" John and Carl wanted to ride, too. Mrs. Young's class will never forget the special day on the farm.

Page 49

1. alone, known
2. bowl, roll
3. coat, wrote
4. home, roam
5. mail, bale
6. maid, frayed
7. plate, great
8. seize, bees
9. sigh, fly
10. soap, rope

Page 50

1. cane
2. site
3. cape
4. tube
5. dote
6. note
7. rate
8. lobe
9. bite
10. cube
11. grime
12. fine
13. bathe
14. vane
15. plane

Page 52

1. D
2. A
3. B
4. D

Page 53

1. 3/10
2. 1/2
3. 5/6
4. 5/8
5. 4/7
6. 1/2

Page 55

O	C	E	N	C	O	N	T	I	N	O	N	T	S	E	A
A	N	T	A	R	C	T	I	C	A	N	C	E	A	E	C
N	S	E	E	R	E	M	A	M	I	C	R	A	E	U	I
T	R	I	S	T	A	S	S	A	D	R	M	T	M	R	R
I	C	C	A	O	M	B	L	U	N	E	Y	L	A	O	E
C	B	I	N	P	A	C	I	F	I	C	A	A	E	P	M
M	E	D	I	T	E	R	R	A	N	E	A	N	S	E	A
A	R	S	H	N	M	N	M	N	N	A	R	T	K	K	H
E	I	A	C	K	C	A	L	P	U	S	R	I	C	A	T
S	N	P	H	L	A	R	C	T	I	C	E	C	A	S	R
D	G	O	T	B	A	C	K	I	M	R	A	A	L	E	O
E	S	O	U	T	H	A	M	E	R	I	C	A	B	A	N
R	E	T	O	O	C	I	X	E	M	F	O	F	L	U	G
M	A	U	S	T	R	A	L	I	A	P	A	T	O	T	O

Page 56

1. 3:45
2. 4:15
3. 10:50
4. 6:05
5. 6:10
6. 6:00
7. 5:55
8. 1:45
9. 2:35

Page 57

1. P.M.
2. A.M.
3. P.M.
4. P.M.
5. A.M.
6. A.M.
7. P.M.
8. P.M.
9. P.M.
10. A.M.
11. A.M.
12. P.M.

Page 58

1. 24
2. 4,251
3. 8,854
4. 75
5. 5,117
6. 842

Page 59

1. 1/3
2. 1/4
3. 5/6
4. 4/6
5. 7/10
6. 2/6
7. 3/4
8. 1/2

This Award Is Presented To

____

for

- ★ Doing Your Best
- ★ Trying Hard
- ★ Not Giving Up
- ★ Making a Great Effort